# GNOSIS MANAGEMENT
## 8 Mistakes Managers Make
### A Quick Reference

# GNOSIS MANAGEMENT
## 8 Mistakes Managers Make
### A Quick Reference

---

By
Anthony Lavonne

Any similarity with real persons in this book is purely coincidental.

## DEDICATION
TO THOSE WHO SEEK SUCCESS FOR THEMSELVES, THE
COMPANY THEY WORK FOR AND THEIR EMPLOYEES.

# TABLE OF CONTENTS

# INTRODUCTION

This book can be used by managers of all levels, in large or small groups and as individual study to help promote ideas for effective leadership in the organization. The book can also be used by those desiring to become a manager by helping prepare them for the responsibilities of management.

Now for a little about me and what this book is really about. I have worked for a small startup and billion dollar companies. Some companies were privately held and others publically traded. I have a college degree in business from a reputable school and have been in the workplace now for over two decades.

I'm not a Vice President or CEO. I have held positions such as Manager, Sr. Manager and Director. However, what qualifies me to write this book is that above all else, I have been a subordinate employee—if there really is such a thing—reporting to managers such as you.

Whether I have been a manager or an individual contributor, I have seen good and bad management styles. I have been in positions where I loved going to work and performed very well as a result. I have also had positions that I dreaded and felt Corporate Post Traumatic Stress Disorder (CPTSD as I call it), fearing my manager and waiting for the next firestorm.

Of course, this book is all subject to my opinion and experience. I write about what I have seen as effective and ineffective management. There may be other styles that provide results, but I find the solutions presented in this book to be a foundation for good management style and practice and will work for broad groups of businesses and employees.

I honestly believe if managers avoid the mistakes mentioned in this book and apply the provided solutions, employees will be happier and companies will have increasing profits.

Tony Lavonne

# WHERE'S THE DATA
## (The Magic Wand Approach or Omniscient Syndrome)

### HERE'S THE PROBLEM

I remember when I was working on my degree in business and the instructors would show all kinds of data points to illustrate trends, gaps, and processes. They explained how to gather the data, how to evaluate the data and that by evaluating the data in different ways you can make proper business decisions. I thought how cool that was, to be able to take data points and have the results of those data points enable you to make good business decisions.

In the business world, there are some areas that have very strict rules about data and its uses. Some of those areas are accounting and finance. If you break the rules there, you can report erroneous financial results and may possibly even get jail time.

However, in many other areas of business I have noticed that often the data is absent and that many of those in top management positions don't even know what data they need and how to analyze it.

They go off their gut feelings. I call this the omniscient syndrome or the magic wand approach. They think because they are in a position of authority they know what to do and that the data doesn't matter. They are in control, they are in authority and the world will follow.

I saw this firsthand at more than one company. I remember an experience where the president of the company I worked for had decided that we would not enter a new market. That may not seem bad in and of its self, as resources may be short and a specific focus can be good for business. However, in this situation the new market was clearly replacing the existing market that we were in. The data showed this was the case. The president made the comment the world would stay with us. In other words, he thought we were the market and not that we were a player within the market. I remember marveling at the arrogance and knew the company would suffer.

In less than a year, profits for the company were dropping fast and market share was tumbling faster than anyone dared look. The president realized his mistake, but it was too late. He changed direction realizing we needed to enter the new market. It took significant effort to get the product ready. Because the product was being rushed to gain market entry as soon as possible, when it finally was released it was full of problems and customers continued to leave and were losing faith in the company. This had been a company known for its quality products and customer service. It wasn't long before the once dominant position the company held fell to a pittance of its former glory. With that fall came tumbling profits and the loss of many jobs.

In another company that was losing sales fast, I saw the omniscient syndrome again. The company had several products; one of them was a cash cow that had brought the company passed the billion dollar mark. Over time, other products began to emerge that filled the same space as the one that had brought the company so much success in the past. During this time the CEO was trying to expand the product line with products that could replace the cash cow product, which was no longer a cash cow. I remember this CEO being dismissed because of his strategy, at least that's how it looked to many of us. The Chairman of the Board got up and delivered a speech explaining the product that had brought the company so much success in the past was not dying and was not dead. It had a long life or long legs as he would say. He went on to explain that he knew this because he had a relative that continued to use the product and thought it was great.

I was amazed that someone of this man's influence and education appeared to be unaware of product life cycles. Generally, products grow, level off and then decline. His sole data point–at least that he mentioned to hundreds of employees–was a relative who used the declining product. As a result, the product continued to decline and profits became just a shadow of what they had been.

In still another company, there was a move into international territories that the data showed would not be profitable. In this case, the company had engaged an outside company to provide a market assessment. From what I was told, the assessment showed that we would not be successful.

However, I was told the CEO had a personal friend and valued customer that wanted the company to expand into that particular region, so we did. The company constantly lost money each month as dollars were spent to keep a market open that was not profitable. In this case, the data was ignored and it was thought the magic wand of success would make things right.

Eventually, this once large and successful company lost so much money they were essentially sold off for their assets.

HERE'S THE SOLUTION
I believe that in the examples provided above, the disasters could have been avoided or at least significantly curtailed if the proper data had been gathered and analyzed. The analysis could then have been used to help make wise decisions. This won't guarantee success, but it can go a long way in identifying a specific problem and also current success areas. Sometimes it is just as important to know what you are doing right as it is in identifying the problem.

I have seen simple diagnostic tools like trend charts, fishbone diagrams and control charts reveal valuable information. Six Sigma, if properly used can help many companies with data analysis. But you don't have to use Six Sigma to use and analyze data. I mention it only as an option. Proper data analysis can be used in many areas to enhance the decision making process.

# Not Listening

## (The Blinders of Management)

### Here's the Problem

Sometimes you may reprimand an employee because timelines are not met, or the work was not done according to your expectations. It appears to the manager the evidence is all in–the work is not done! Besides, it is the end results that matter and not the in-between things. There may be some higher ups that are putting pressure on you, reiterating that money is being lost and budgets are out of control.

### Here's the Solution

There is always more to the story than can be seen. For example, an employee is working through a project, but requires the help of people in other departments or groups throughout the company to accomplish the required tasks. Because the other people are required for the project, it cannot be completed without their help. The other people do not report to the employee who is responsible for the project and the managers of the other people keep pulling their people off to do other "more important" work.

You should take the time to listen, to allow the employee to explain in their own words how the project is going, what obstacles are being encountered and what can be improved. Often the employee knows exactly what needs to happen to have the project put back on track, but lacks the support or "power" needed to get it done. Sometimes they may need guidance as they explain the hurdles they are encountering. It might just be, you can help the success of the project by helping remove the bottlenecks the employee is encountering, but if you don't know what they are you cannot understand what needs to happen and help facilitate a solution.

In the situation described above, listening is essential to the success of the project. If you just reprimanded the employee and tell them they better get the project finished, the employee may feel they are in an impossible situation. They can't satisfy you and they cannot finish the project. Then the employee may spend more time worrying about their job and less on the required project. In that situation the company and the employee lose.

# DICTATING *VS.* FACILITATING
## (THE HELPING HAND APPROACH)

### HERE'S THE PROBLEM

Some employees' dream of the day they can give the orders and others have to follow. I heard how a director was told by their supervisor that they were a director and they should direct. They meant, you tell the employee what to do and they do it. Little did the supervisor of the director know that his director's team was the most productive in the department and it was because of the director's management style of being a facilitator rather than a dictator?

In another situation I witnessed, I saw a top level executive run his department with an iron fist. This executive held a daily meeting with his managers that took one and a half to two hours every morning. During this meeting he would dictate what the managers were to do that day. He made the statement that he was the decision maker and that there did not need to be a consensus to get the work done. He disliked a collaborative approach to decisions and felt he had all the knowledge necessary to make the correct decisions. After all, he wouldn't be in an executive position if he didn't have the answers.

### HERE'S THE SOLUTION

Usually, a manager does not have all of the skills necessary to do the jobs of those who report to him or her. Just because they manage an employee does not mean they are all knowing about that employee's job. If they dictate everything, they may more easily step into a micromanagement situation, which no employee appreciates. It causes the employee to second guess everything they do and shows a lack of trust on the manager's part. Generally speaking, you will see more employees leave that kind of situation because of how uncomfortable it is and because they cannot use their already acquired skills.

You are a manager most likely because you know how to get things done and get them done right. The best use of your talents is to facilitate the success of your employees by seeing they have what they need to get the job done, not by playing dictator. Hopefully, you have hired well and your people already have the skills for the job—trust that expertise and experience. If you don't, you will not be able to tap into the rich resources your employee can offer and they will leave you and the company and find a place where they can use their talents.

As a facilitator you help your employee by busting down roadblocks for them, providing advice and seeing the employee has the proper tools to get the job done. If you will do these things, the employee will be more likely to succeed and their success will contribute to the success of the company and you as the manager.

# SHORTSIGHTEDNESS
## (The Myopia of Tumbling Profits)

HERE'S THE PROBLEM

Because we live in a society that expects growth in business and the economy in general, growth is expected–even in the short-term. If we don't get it, we are targeted and not for good. This causes many of those in the position of directing companies to focus on the short-term. It is good to focus on the short-term, but not at the expense of the long-term success of the company.

Sure, I can have the nice, sweet cinnamon roll today, but I may pay for it with a heart attack in the long-term. Of course, if you plan on only being with a company a short time, you may not care. If we all took that approach to business, most businesses would fail and that affects everybody, including you.

Here is a classic example; I have noticed a specific trend in the corporate world when it comes to cutting budgets. That is to perform layoffs, sometimes resulting in a large reduction in force. This is especially true of public companies. The executives have to satisfy the stockholders or their jobs are on the line. One very visible way to show action is to do layoffs. Now, I admit that layoffs may be necessary, but I have seen some layoffs actually cost the company a great deal of money. Enough money that the advertised savings were greatly inflated because the cost of losing the employees were never calculated (here we go with data again). The cost can be measured in money and knowledge.

HERE'S THE SOLUTION

When making short-term decisions, look at the long-term effects. If you see a downside in the long-term, look for ways to counter the potential issues. If not, you are waving that magic wand again and throwing the company to the wind.

At least quarterly, look at the short-term, mid-term and long term situations looming on the horizon (i.e. short-term is the quarter, mid-term is semi-annually and the longer term one to three years). Most companies have sales goals they set every year and then determine what needs to be met each quarter to reach the annual goal. During this process, take the time to see what can affect the company in a negative manner if you stay on the same course. You should look at market conditions, employee loss or recruitment and the economy to name a few. Often the economy is ignored and considered a constant when looking at goals. This can be dangerous in keeping step with the reality of things. You will have specifics for your company and industry that you should evaluate. Remember look at and use the data!

Before layoffs are considered the cure-all, make sure you understand the ramifications of such actions:

Such as:
- The Loss of Irreplaceable Experts: Some employees are the company. What am I going to lose that cannot be replaced. A body can survive without the arm; albeit less effectively, but absolutely needs the head. Do you know what the parts are to the company and how its body functions? If you cut off the wrong part, the damage may be irreparable.
- Employee Loyalty: An employee is a person with goals, hobbies and often families. When layoffs take place, the company is sending a very clear message to the departing employee. We don't care about you! We can get the job done without you! You are a cog in a wheel! The important part to remember here is that it is not just the employee who we are

booting out the door that feels this way, these feelings also transfers to the existing workforce. Some questions to answer before taking the drastic measure of a layoff is how the layoff will affect remaining employees? How many will leave of their own freewill because they no longer trust the company? Will I loose essential expertise with the backlash of exiting employees? The answer is probably yes. Can you afford the loss?

# MICROMANAGING
## (MY WAY OR THE HIGHWAY)

HERE'S THE PROBLEM

We talked a little about this in the *Dictating vs. Facilitating* chapter; now let's expand on this as we discuss the topic of micromanaging.

I remember being a first time manager. I had a team of 22 people that reported to me. They were very loyal, had great expertise and got the job done. It was a team that other employees sought to become a part of. After a while, I was given a new responsibility. The company chose someone out of the team to fill the manager role I had held. My replacement had always done what was required of him and did it with a good attitude and extraordinary skill. However, when he took over as manager a different person emerged. The once, nice, friendly and compliant employee turned into a reining tyrant.

This manager tried to manage all of his employee's work, right down to the tiniest detail. It took so much of his time that he could not possibly work with all 22 people in an effective manner. The team didn't dare make a move without him. The once productive team became inefficient, not daring to make a move without the manager telling them to. In addition, employee complaints went up and stress was so high that the once productive team was now falling apart very quickly.

Here is another experience. I remember working at a company where the CEO made an announcement. He said that he had been standing at his window the past few weeks watching employees arrive at the workplace. He said that many were not walking fast enough. He said you should look excited to get to work. He mentioned that some people arrived after 8:00 in the morning. He then announced new core business hours that all employees were required to follow. From that day forward, all employees were required to be at work from 8:00 to 5:00 as the standard core hours—no exceptions.

Now I had been at companies that had core hours before, but they allowed flexibility at the beginning and end of the day. Some core hours were required for meetings and proper business contact.

The Backlash of the announcement was tremendous. People that had been putting in extra time, some coming in at 9:00 or 10:00 in the morning and leaving at 10:00 at night decided to only put in the required time. Rather than productivity going up, it went down significantly and soured the attitude of a large population of employees.

Also, telling someone to be happy when coming to work is not the answer to happiness on the job. The right conditions need to be in place and usually that means flexibility, the opposite of what was being fostered in this situation.

I have to admit, that I also decided to put in the exact hours and then go home. I had been arriving at 8:00 and leaving around 6:00, but was dismayed by the request and rebelled in my own quiet manner.

HERE'S THE SOLUTION
Respect your employees. Respect does not mean the employee is not accountable. Effective accountability is essential and can be obtained with regular reports, or one-on-one meetings. This also gives you as the manager a chance to play the role of facilitator.

Allow your employees to get the job done their way—as long as it works. Many managers feel like they are a manager because their way is "thee" way of doing things. Remember, $6 + 6 = 12$, $4 \times 3 = 12$ and $6 \times 2 = 12$. All the equations provide the same results. You might be a $6 \times 2$ person and your employee a $4 \times 3$ person. If you force them

to be a 6 x 2 person they may be less productive. Look to the end results of the employee's work and facilitate the process. Does it really matter what time the employee gets to work, or how much time they put in, whether they work from home or the office? In some cases it might make a difference, but the point should be the end results and not the in-between things.

# Too Many Hours & Unrealistic Expectations
## (The Hidden bondage of Corporate Culture)

### Here's the Problem

How many times do you hear a friend, family member or neighbor complain about the work hours they are putting in and the workplace's unrealistic expectations on their time? The corporate world has radically changed in the last couple of decades when it comes to the demands on an employee's time.

A couple of years ago, I was sitting in a meeting where a director was conducting a meeting with his team. I was not part of the team, but was attending due to some of the content that would be discussed during the course of the meeting.

The director in a very stern voice told his team that the reason the company paid each of their cell phone bills was so that each member of his team could be leashed to their phone 24 hours a day 7 days a week. He actually used the word leashed. He then spent another five minutes elaborating on this topic.

The team being addressed was not a team that provided emergency support, but could occasionally be contacted for their expertise during off hours. They also spent some time traveling which required special cell phone accounts. They were exempt employees, so no overtime was paid when contacted after hours. I thought it quite interesting that paying approximately 110 dollars a month for a cell phone bill provided the company with 24 by 7 access. Pretty good deal for the company I would say.

In another situation, I saw a team of people that were often called upon after hours, putting in 60 to 80 hour weeks in some cases. Yet, when it came to time off the employee had to use their vacation time and the extra hours they put in were chalked up to the job.

I spoke to a co-worker one time and she shared with me some good news. She told me that her husband had a new job. She then told me why it was such a relief to get him out of the place he was at and into a new environment.

Her husband was a database administrator (a DBA) that supported several clients. If there was a problem with the database, he could be called upon at any time to remedy the situation. Because there were regular issues, he spent many off hours working. His wife told me that her husband didn't even dare go to the store or to the bathroom in some cases; for fear that he would get a call. He was essentially a slave in a free country.

What is interesting about this situation is the company he was working for had hired specific DBA's for afterhours coverage, but let them all go to save money. Now the company was going to lose their only expert for the specific databases he covered. I wonder how much that cost?

HERE'S THE SOLUTION
When an employer is not respectful of an employee's time, the employee may get burned out, disgruntled and eventually leave the company. Forcing the company to then hire someone who most likely will need to be retrained and take some time to get up to speed with the new surroundings and inner-workings of the company.

If an employee puts in extra time, let them take some comp time (compensatory time) that does not come out of vacation time off and don't make them feel guilty for taking the time.

If contact by cell phone is required afterhours, only make contact when it is truly needed. If possible, provide a rotation schedule among employees so they know when they truly have free time and when they need to listen for an incoming work related call.

Don't inundate an employee with e-mail after hours unless immediate attention is required or you have set the bar beforehand letting the employee know they do not need to respond to e-mail at all hours of the day, that you will call or text them in emergency situations.

# PUNISHING FOR MISTAKES
## (THE GARBAGE CAN OF PREVENTION)

### HERE'S THE PROBLEM

I remember having a conversation with the company CIO about an employee that had mishandled her laptop and as a result the laptop was stolen. There was an investigation to see if business would be affected by the data on the laptop. Sufficient security measures were in place that protected the data on the laptop, so the risk was deemed minimal.

As I discussed this with the CIO, he commented that the employee should probably be fired. That particular employee was not in his department, so he could not fire her. I then said to him, that if they keep her on she will never make that mistake again and if they hire a new person, the new person may also have to learn the lesson the hard way. He seemed a little surprised by my response.

Oftentimes, you will see employees that are more interested in protecting themselves than in the affect their actions might have on the company. As long as I can prove that someone else is responsible, the safer I am.

This type of mentality is often caused because companies punish for mistakes that can be learned from, changes made and provide more success for the company down the road.

In an environment where everyone is trying to cover themselves, mistakes can more easily take place or the real problems hidden from view.

In one company I witnessed an executive that in his staff meeting would yell and scream—literally—at people for making mistakes. He would threaten their jobs or their promotion possibilities and would do this often. He ruled by fear. The problem with ruling by fear is that people are thinking in the back of their mind while they are working on something about how to protect themselves, rather than on how best to do the work.

## HERE'S THE SOLUTION

I remember in my university finance class they taught us that a sunk cost was sunk; meaning, that if a company had spent a great deal of money on something, the money spent was gone. You had to look at the future cost and not the past cost. At least, that is how I remember it.

In any case, I think that philosophy applies here too. Don't look at the mistake in the past, look at what needs to be changed in the future. The past has happened and firing someone or punishing them will not repair what has happened in most cases. The decisions should be based on the future effects.

# The CEO is Always Right
## (The Dictatorship of the Corporate Hierarchy)

I find it fascinating how employees will do anything a CEO says, because he is the CEO. This can go for any manager position in the corporate hierarchy.

Currently, in the United States some people fear they are losing their freedoms. I'm not saying that is or is not a correct assessment. Some feel they have less say in how things are run in the country and have more restrictions on what they can do. As a result, the dissatisfied citizen will sometimes verbalize their dissatisfaction to those around them because of the fear of losing more freedoms.

Yet, this same person will go to work and willingly submit to what can be referred to as the dictatorship of the corporate hierarchy. If an executive makes a decision, the employees are expected to obey. If they do not, the employee most likely will not keep their job. It doesn't matter if the decision makes sense or not. Now, I am not advocating rebellion in the workplace. Remember, this book is written for managers. I understand the importance of a final say in things. However, this final say should have logical support, not just command support for its action to be successful.

I remember when a Sr. Director was evaluating some work that needed to be done. All of the managers underneath him and all of the employees of those managers felt like the company was losing a lot of money because of an inefficient process. This process was handled by an application that ran a specific job or jobs against a database to create orders and charge customers by the thousands every night.

The problem was the job would often fail and orders would get mixed up or maybe taxed inappropriately. Sometimes there would be wrong charges placed against credit cards and this would result in extra fees to get fixed. The problem caused many man hours of work to correct on at least a weekly basis, sometimes more. Most of the time the fixes were done late at night or over the weekend and involved the time of many employees. The employee that managed the process would go to work for eight hours and then monitor the job for three to four hours every night.

The Sr. Director didn't want to have his employees spend their time working on something that did not have visibility beyond the Information Technology Department. He knew that his people would always fix things. However, his employees knew the human and corporate costs associated with the inefficient application were significant.

It did not matter to the Sr. Director how many employees believed the application needed to be fixed. His one opinion outweighed all the others because he was the boss.

In this case eventually the work was done and it resulted in significant savings to the company and much higher employee satisfaction. However, many experts in the area were being overruled by one voice, a voice that did not deal directly with the problems at hand.

HERE'S THE SOLUTION
This type of hierarchal governance can be costly to a company if used inappropriately. Of course, there needs to be order and one way to do that is through a hierarchal structure.

A good manager will entertain the opinion of his experts and realize that he or she should be able to show the logic of any decision made.

I remember one time when an employee of mine disagreed with me on a software development project. One of his first statements to me was that I can just tell him what to do, even if he doesn't agree.

I told him that I should have to show the logic of my approach, just as he should. We spent the next 30 minutes going over the logic of each other's proposal. In the end, the employee and I were in total agreement on what needed to be done and when the project was implemented it was a success.

This collaborative process allows the best fruits to float to the top. However, I have found the collaborative approach works best in small groups and one-on-one situations where everyone can be open and cover each topic at hand adequately. Too many people can often bring too many opinions to get anything accomplished. Generally, those who work directly with the subject matter would be included in such decisions.

# REVIEW

- Use data analysis. Use the data to help make wise decisions.
- Listen to your employees: Understand their roadblocks and their ideas for success.
- Be a facilitator. By listening to your employee you can understand where you can help remove roadblocks or offer other help in getting their work done.
- Look at the long-term as well as the short-term. Consider the medium and long-term ramifications of any decisions; particularly, fiscal decisions.
- Use your employee's experience and expertise. Don't get caught up on the in-between things. There is often more than one way to get to the end result. What works for one may not work for another. Let the employee do the job their way and focus on the end results.
- Respect your employee's time and limit afterhours contact.
- A sunk cost is sunk. Focus on fixing errors of the past in the future, without necessarily punishing for the past. Punishing can make employees prone to error and try and place blame somewhere else or even cover errors up.
- Use the opinions of those around you. Allow collaboration between you and your employees and the best ideas will float to the top. Don't assume you know best because you are in charge.

www.ingramcontent.com/pod-product-compliance
Lightning Source LLC
Chambersburg PA
CBHW061229180526
45170CB00003B/1218